FOREST FIREFIGHTER

By William David Thomas

Reading Consultant: Susan Nations, M.Ed.,
author/literacy coach/consultant in literacy development

Gareth Stevens
Publishing

Please visit our web site at **www.garethstevens.com**.
For a free catalog describing Gareth Stevens Publishing's list of high-quality books, call 1-800-542-2595 (USA) or 1-800-387-3178 (Canada).
Gareth Stevens Publishing's fax: 1-877-542-2596

Library of Congress Cataloging-in-Publication Data

Thomas, William David.
   Forest Firefighter / William David Thomas.
       p. cm.—(Cool careers. Adventure careers)
    Includes bibliographical references and index.
    ISBN-10: 0-8368-8882-0 ISBN-13: 978-0-8368-8882-9 (lib. bdg.)
    ISBN-10: 0-8368-8889-8 ISBN-13: 978-0-8368-8889-8 (softcover)
    1. Forest fire fighters—Juvenile literature. 2. Fire extinction—
Vocational guidance—Juvenile literature. I. Title.
   SD421.23.T46 2007
   363.37023—dc22   2007027506

This edition first published in 2008 by
Gareth Stevens Publishing
A Weekly Reader® Company
1 Reader's Digest Road
Pleasantville, NY 10570-7000 USA

Copyright © 2008 by Gareth Stevens, Inc.

Senior Managing Editor: Lisa M. Guidone
Managing Editor: Valerie J. Weber
Creative Director: Lisa Donovan
Designer: Paula Jo Smith
Cover Photo Researcher: Kimberly Babbitt
Interior Photo Researcher: Susan Anderson

Picture credits: Cover, title page © Reuters/Corbis; pp. 4–5 © Reuters/Corbis; pp. 6–7 U.S. Forest Service/Missoula Technology and Development Center; p. 8 The Pioneer-Monte Draper/AP; p. 10 Myung J. Chun/LA Times; p. 12 © Kai Forsterling/epa/Corbis; p. 13 Paula Jo Smith; pp. 14–15 © Raymond Gehman/Corbis; p. 16 B. Brindle/Snow & Neally; p. 17 Sam Mircovich/Reuters/Corbis; pp. 18–19 © Ed Kashi/Corbis; pp. 20–21 © Yves Forestier/Corbis; pp. 22–23 © Pablo Otin/epa/Corbis; pp. 24–25, 27 Mike McMillan/Spotfire Images; p. 29 © Kevin R. Morris/Corbis

Printed in the United States of America

1 2 3 4 5 6 7 8 9 10 09 08 07

CONTENTS

Words in the glossary appear in **bold** type the first time they are used in the text.

CHAPTER 1
SUMMERS OF DANGER

Thick smoke makes it hard to breathe. You're tired, but you swing the sharp tool again and again. The blade cuts through roots and branches. You clear them away, then dig up the soil and turn it over. Nearby, a chainsaw rattles and whines. Someone yells, "**Swamper** here!" You run toward her. You grab one end of the log she has cut and help carry it into the forest. Then it's back to chopping, digging, and turning the soil.

You turn and see the fire moving closer to you. You can feel the heat. Your eyes and throat burn from the smoke. Every muscle in your body is sore, but you can't stop. You are fighting to save a forest. You are fighting to save your own life. You're battling a raging forest fire.

A towering wall of flames roars through a forest in Colorado. Brave, specially trained forest firefighters will try to stop it.

Becoming a Forest Firefighter

A writer once said a big forest fire is like "a hurricane of flames." Fighting fires is a hard and dangerous job. Fires can injure or kill people who get near them. Every summer, brave men and women go into rugged forests and mountains to stop these fires. Not everyone can be a firefighter. You have to be strong and very physically fit. You must pass a **fitness** test just to get into a training program. The U.S. Forest Service runs these programs. This federal agency manages public lands in national forests and grasslands.

If you want to watch for fires and fight them on the ground, you must go through this training. Pilots also receive specific training. Are you willing to jump from a plane to reach faraway forest fires? If so, you must attend a special school for smoke jumpers.

In these Forest Service classes, you will learn how to use firefighting tools. You are also taught how fires start and how fires act. You must learn first aid and how to read maps and use radios. You will learn how the land, wind, and weather affect fires. Some training is done in classrooms, and some occurs in the forest.

Most firefighters work only during the fire season, from May through October. A few firefighters work all year long. In winter, they check and repair equipment. They may patrol forests on skis or snowshoes. They look for places where fires might start in the summer.

Most firefighters love to be outdoors. One of the reasons they fight fires is to preserve forests. They want to protect the land and the animals that live there. Every summer, they risk their lives to do it.

A firefighter opens an emergency shelter and crawls inside. These fireproof, **heat-resistant** shelters can save lives in a fire.

CHAPTER 2
THE WATCHERS

National parks and forests are huge. In many parts, there are no roads or buildings. Fires often start in these faraway places. A fire can grow really big before anyone knows about it.

Spotting forest fires when they are small is the job of the watchers. They may also be called fire spotters or lookouts. **Foresters** know they are the first line of defense against fires.

Eye in the Sky

Watchers work in fire towers built on the tops of high hills. The towers need to be taller than the trees

The sun casts a glow on this fire tower in Bemidji, Minnesota. The tower is used for fire watching.

around them. They may be as high as 90 feet (27 meters). Fire watchers are stationed in these towers from May to October.

The top of a fire tower is enclosed. Large
windows on all sides provide a clear view across the
forest. Sometimes a balcony or a **catwalk** circles the
outside. Watchers spend all day in the tower
looking for smoke. They use binoculars to help
them see more clearly.

If smoke is spotted, the watcher uses maps, a
compass, and other tools to locate the fire. He
or she marks the place on a map, then calls fire
headquarters. Managers there may call other
fire towers. They will ask if other watchers can
see the smoke too. A spotter plane may be sent
to fly over the area. The pilot, too, will look for
smoke. Once the exact location of the fire is
known, crews can be sent out to fight it.

Three Kinds of Fires

There are three kinds of forest fires: ground,
surface, and crown. Ground fires burn roots and
other material under the soil. These fires can
travel a long way underground. At any time,
they may rise up and burn aboveground. Ground
fires are hard to find and put out. Surface fires
burn above ground. Their fuel is grass, shrubs,
logs, and trees. In a big surface fire, flames may
rise 300 feet (91 m) into the air. Crown fires
burn in the tops of trees and are very dangerous.
They can move fast and may spread quickly from
one place to another.

Lonely Danger

Most watchers live alone in small cabins. These homes are usually built near the bottom of a tower. Food, water, and mail are sent out to the tower every two or three weeks. The watcher may have to hike to the nearest road to get these supplies. Then he or she must carry them to the tower in a backpack. A watcher may not see another person for a long time. It's a lonely job, and it can be dangerous.

Finding the exact location of a fire is very important. This watcher is using an azimuth indicator — a fire finder — to do the job right.

The biggest danger is being caught in a fire. Fires can spread fast. If a fire is nearby, a watcher may stay in the tower and send reports. Usually the watcher will move to a safer place.

There are other dangers, too. One fire spotter in New York told how he had been trapped in his tower for two days. Bears were prowling around his cabin looking for food. He could not come down until the bears went away.

Lightning is one of the greatest dangers for watchers. Forest Service workers tell about a fire watcher out West. On his first day of work, lightning hit his tower. All of the windows blew in, and the young fire spotter was knocked out. When he woke up, he brushed broken glass from his hair and clothes. Then he climbed down the ladder, walked away from the tower, and never came back. Fortunately, most fire watchers stick with the job longer than that!

The Fire Finder

One of the tools watchers use is an azimuth indicator. It combines a **sight** with a round map and a compass. If a spotter sees smoke, he or she lines it up in the sight. The indicator tells the watcher how far away the smoke is. It helps the watcher find the fire's location on the map. A forest ranger named William Osborne made the first tool like this in 1910. He called it a "fire finder."

CHAPTER 3

THE HOT SHOTS

A forest ranger once said, "You can always tell which ones they are. They're the folks with no eyebrows." He was talking about hot shots. These are the men and women who walk on burning ground. With courage and an ax, they take on forest fires face-to-face.

A special mask helps this forest firefighter breathe amid smoke, ashes, and dust.

Nightmare

Fighting forest fires is a dangerous business. It can be deadly. Hot shots often work very close to the flames. Burns are common — including lost eyebrows. One slip with a chainsaw or an ax can cause terrible injuries. Burning branches or whole trees can fall without warning.

But the hot shots' greatest worry is called **burnover.** This situation happens when a fire spreads much faster than expected. Firefighters get trapped by flames racing faster than they can run. Burnover is the nightmare of every hot shot.

The Fire Triangle

Three things are needed to make a fire. Fuel, **oxygen**, and heat are called "the fire triangle." If any part of the triangle is taken away, a fire can't burn. Forest firefighters try to break the fire triangle. They clear away trees, branches, and grass in front of a fire. When the fire reaches the cleared area, it has no fuel. Without fuel, the fire goes out.

OXYGEN · HEAT · FUEL

Sawyers and Swampers

Sometimes hot shots get lucky. When a forest fire breaks out near a road, they can ride to it in trucks or jeeps. Most of the time, they have to hike miles through the forest to reach the fire. And they have to carry all of their gear with them. That gear can weigh 45 pounds (20 kilograms) or more for each person.

A crew chief decides how the hot shots will fight the fire. They usually make a firebreak, which is a wide path of bare ground. The hot shots get in front of the fire and start clearing away anything that can burn.

Flames shoot out of a drip torch to start a backfire. This Idaho forest firefighter is using a fast — but dangerous — way to make a firebreak.

Sawyers use chainsaws. They cut down trees and saw fallen logs. Other hot shots cut brush and small trees with hand tools. Swampers pick up the cut material and haul it away from the fire. Then everyone starts to dig. Leaves, pine needles, and roots beneath the soil can burn. All of it has to be removed. When the firebreak is clear, the hot shots move back and watch. They have to be sure the fire doesn't jump across the break.

Hot Equipment

This is some of the gear that hot shots take when they head for a fire.

- Tall, heavy boots
- Hard hat
- Heat-resistant jacket
- Thick gloves
- Backpack
- Radio

- Hand tools like axes
- Chainsaws and fuel
- Food and water
- First-aid kit
- Tiny, fireproof tent

Fighting Fire With Fire

Sometimes hot shots start fires. When there isn't enough time to clear a firebreak with tools, hot shots clear the land by burning it. They call this a backfire. It is dangerous, but sometimes it is the only way to stop a fire.

The hot shots' work isn't over when a fire is stopped. "Mopping up" is a long, dirty job. Crews walk through the burned area looking for "hot spots." These are small areas where the fire may still be burning. Each of them must be put out completely.

Pulaski

In August 1910, Ed Pulaski was leading a crew of hot shots in Idaho. The fire was about to overrun them. Ed led the crew to safety in an old mine. He saved the lives of forty men. But there is more to Ed's story. The next year, he made a tool for fighting fires. It had a two-sided head. One side was an ax blade; the other was a curved hoe for digging. Firefighters across the country soon used the tool, calling it a pulaski. Today, the U.S. Forest Service orders thirty-five thousand pulaskis every year.

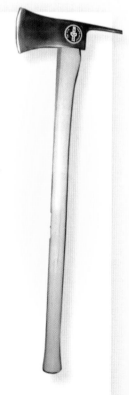

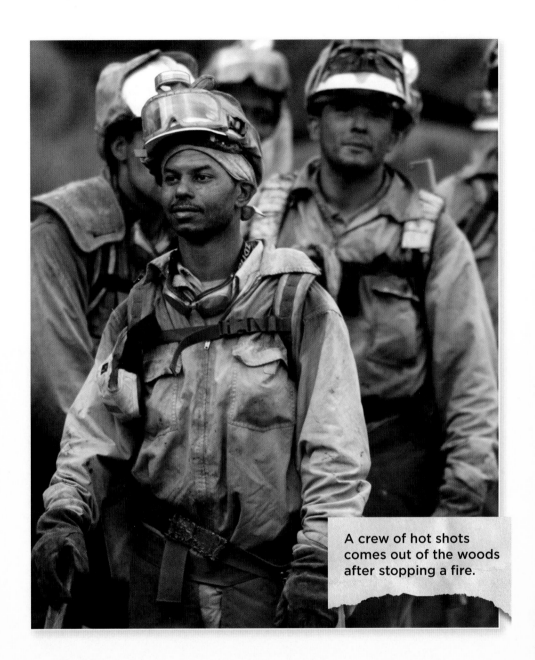

A crew of hot shots comes out of the woods after stopping a fire.

When the hot shots finally head for home, they are sweaty, dirty, and very, very tired. They have to walk out, carrying their gear with them. But when they have stopped a fire, they don't mind the hike. Hot shots call it a victory march.

CHAPTER 4

THE FLYERS

In the movie *Always,* actor Richard Dreyfuss plays a Forest Service pilot. A crew of hot shots is almost trapped by a fire. Dreyfuss flies in and drops **chemicals** to slow the fire. But he flies too low. One of his engines catches fire. A moment later, the airplane explodes.

That scene surprises people watching the movie. It doesn't surprise firefighters. They know the dangers of flying near forest fires. And they know the risks pilots take to stop fires and protect hot shots on the ground.

Choppers and Props

Both the Forest Service and the Parks Service have air bases. The services use helicopters, often called choppers. They also use many kinds of airplanes with propellers, or props. They don't use jet planes, which fly too fast to spot or fight fires.

The services don't teach people how to fly. You must be a licensed pilot first. But all pilots must take special training classes. They have to pass tests—both written and in the air—before they can fly to fires.

A pilot scoops water from a lake to drop on a fire.

A pilot and a spotter check on a fire. They will report its location, size, and movement to crews on the ground.

Spotters

Some pilots work as spotters. They fly over forests, looking for smoke. If they see a fire, they may radio watchers in nearby towers. Working with a watcher on the ground, they can pinpoint the fire's location. Some spotter planes use special **infrared scopes** and cameras. These instruments help pilots find fires in heavy clouds or smoke.

During a fire, spotters fly overhead to see how big it is and in what direction it is moving. But flying near fires is dangerous. In 1988, a helicopter pilot was flying to a huge fire in Yellowstone Park. Flames were leaping 300 feet (91 m) into the air. As he got closer, his helicopter quit moving. The wind made by the fire was so strong, it stopped the aircraft. Even at full power, the pilot could not move forward.

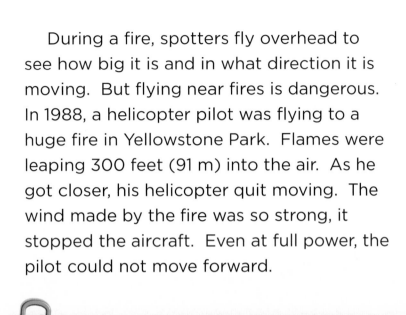

Convection Columns

Warm air weighs less than cool air. Because it weighs less, warm air rises. The air around a fire is hot and rises very quickly. When the hot air rises, cool air rushes in to take its place. Thus, the fire creates its own wind! The wind makes the fire burn even faster.

Sometimes the rising hot air will spin. Scientists call this **convection**. Firefighters call it trouble. The hot, spinning air makes a column of thick smoke. It's called a convection column. It looks like a tornado. On the ground below, the fire is a whirling mass of flames. A convection column is the sign of a very dangerous fire.

Colors in the Forest

Using two-way radios, flyers often talk to hot shots on the ground. The ground crews give directions to the pilots, telling them where to drop special chemicals onto fires. These chemicals slow the fires down or stop them. The chemicals are called **fire retardants**. Wet and sticky, they coat trees and leaves. This coating cools the plants so they are less likely to burn. The retardants are brightly colored—yellow, red, or pink. Pilots can see the color on trees from the air. This lets them know which areas have already been covered.

It's dangerous work. As in the movie *Always,* planes can catch fire. They can also be thrown around by the strong winds that rise from fires. In thick smoke and clouds, pilots can crash into hills or tall trees.

Brightly colored chemicals flow onto a forest fire. To make an accurate drop, the pilot must fly close to the trees and flames.

Flyers carry people and equipment, too. If an open landing area can be found, helicopters carry hot shots to fires. They also deliver food, water, and other supplies to fire crews. And, of course, pilots fly smoke jumpers. These are the crews that parachute into the forest to fight fires.

Burning Money

Wildfires do more than destroy forests. They cost a lot of money, too. Every year, the Forest Service counts the number of forest fires. It also totals the money spent to fight them. Firefighters and their gear cost money. So do pilots, aircraft, and fuel. In 2004, there were more than seventy-seven thousand wildfires in the United States. Fighting these fires costs more than $900 million.

CHAPTER 5

THE SMOKE JUMPERS

Skydivers jump out of airplanes for fun. For them, it's a thrilling hobby, like skiing or kayaking. But when you parachute into a forest fire, it isn't much fun. And it isn't a hobby; it's a job — a very dangerous one.

Trampolines and Towers

Every year, hundreds of men and women apply to smoke-jumpers school. Only about fifty are chosen. In training, they study first aid, **fire behavior,** wind, and weather. They do a lot of running and other exercises. After the first week, there's an exam. It's called the pack-out test. Trainees have to carry a 110-pound (55-kg) pack over a 3-mile (5-km) course in ninety minutes or less. If they pass, they go on to jump training.

A smoke jumper guides her parachute through the smoke to land safely near a big fire.

Believe it or not, the first part of jump training is bouncing on trampolines. Jumping and falling on the trampoline teaches jumpers how to land correctly when they jump from a plane. After that, they move to the training towers. The towers are 30 to 50 feet (9 to 15 m) high. Wearing ropes and harnesses, trainees leap from the top. Here, they learn how to jump and how to pull the guide ropes on a parachute.

After three weeks, they go up in a plane. Everyone makes fifteen practice jumps or more. The first ones are easy jumps into fields. Later, they parachute into rough forests and mountains. By the time training is over, these men and women are smoke jumpers.

Gearing Up

When a fire call comes into a smoke-jumper base, people rush to get into their jumpsuits. These brightly colored suits are fire-retardant. Padding protects jumpers from being hurt by tree limbs and rocks when landing. Jumpers also wear a helmet with a face mask.

Each smoke jumper wears two parachutes. The main "chute" is on their back. A smaller, emergency chute is strapped to their stomach. If the main chute doesn't open, this second chute is a backup. Firefighting tools are loaded into gear bags. The bags get parachutes, too.

Jump!

The jumpers file onto the plane and sit on benches. The plane takes off and speeds toward the fire. The pilot looks for a clear **drop zone,** an area where the jumpers can land safely. If a clearing can't be found, the crew has to jump into the forest. One at a time, the jumpers stand in the door of the plane. The jumpmaster signals them to go with a shout or a slap. The first to jump is always the crew chief.

On the way down, parachutes often get caught in trees. The jumper may be stuck dangling high above the ground. Smoke jumpers carry special ropes called safety ladders. If they get caught, they hook these ladders to the tree or the parachute, then climb down.

With their parachutes strapped on and their gear in hand, smoke jumpers head to battle a fire.

On the ground, the crew chief watches to make sure the whole crew lands safely. If the crew is large, the plane may have to make several passes, dropping a few jumpers each time. The plane makes a final pass or two, and the jumpmaster pushes all of the firefighting gear out the door. Bags full of hard hats, gloves, chainsaws, and pulaskis parachute to the ground. The smoke jumpers collect their tools. They are now hot shots, and they rush to stop the fire.

Afterward, the jumpers pack up their gear. It was parachuted in, but it has to be carried out on their backs. They don't mind the hike so much if they have beaten the fire. For the smoke jumpers, like the hot shots, this is a victory march.

A Team Adventure

From spring to fall, the fire watchers, hot shots, flyers, and smoke jumpers work together. Each one has a part in protecting the forests. Watchers in towers keep their eyes open for smoke. They talk to pilots flying spotter planes high above the forests. Both talk to hot shots who are battling fires on the ground. Smoke jumpers dive from the sky and become hot shots themselves. Pilots fly low to drop fire-stopping chemicals into the trees. All of these jobs are dangerous. The men and women doing them work hard — and often risk their lives to preserve our forests. Their work is more than just a job. It's an adventure.

Thirteen Names

In Montana, there is a steep canyon called Mann Gulch. Above it is a hill covered with grass and small trees. Hidden in the grass stand thirteen markers. Each one bears the name of a firefighter. In August 1949, a fire broke out in Mann Gulch. A crew of smoke jumpers parachuted in to fight it. Suddenly, the fire jumped across the canyon and raced toward the men. One by one, the fire caught the smoke jumpers. Afterward, the Forest Service started fire-science laboratories. There, people study fires. They hope to prevent disasters like the one in Mann Gulch.

Future smoke jumpers practice on a tower at a U.S. Forest Service training center in Missoula, Montana.

New Ideas in Forest Management

Experts once thought all fires should be put out quickly. Now they have new ideas. Scientists know that small fires and some logging can help forests grow. Small fires burn dead trees first, clearing the land for new growth. Fires also help spread seeds from which new trees may grow. Trees that grow very close to each other are small. These trees are often weak and burn more easily. Getting rid of some of them allows the other trees to grow bigger and stronger. Large, strong trees don't burn as easily.

Now when a fire starts, firefighters may not try to put it out. They will try to keep it small but let it burn. Controlled fires and controlled logging are now part of forest management.

GLOSSARY

burnover — when a fast-moving forest fire catches firefighters and burns right over the ground they are on

catwalk — a narrow walkway, usually high up on a building

chemicals — elements or materials made by combining elements

compass — a small tool used to find directions

convection — a circular, upward motion in liquids or gases, caused by heat

drop zone — the area where parachutists try to land on the ground

fire behavior — the speed and direction of a fire and how and what it is burning

fire retardants — chemicals that cover objects and make it difficult to burn them

fitness — strength, speed, flexibility, and endurance

foresters — people who plant, cut, and care for trees

heat-resistant — able to keep someone or something safe from heat

infrared scopes — instruments used to find or measure sources of heat

oxygen — a colorless, odorless gas that is part of our air; fires need oxygen to burn

sawyers — people who cut trees with saws

sight — a device used to guide the eye in aiming or figuring out direction, on an instrument or a gun

swamper — on a fire crew, a person who clears away trees and brush cut by sawyers

TO FIND OUT MORE

Books

Forest Fires. High Interest Books (series). Luke Thompson (Children's Press)

Smokejumpers. Elaine Landau (Lerner Publishing Group)

Wildfire. Taylor Morrison (Walter Lorraine Books)

Wildfires. Seymour Simon (HarperCollins Publishers)

Web Sites

Federal Emergency Management Agency
www.fema.gov/kids/index.htm
> Click on the links to find out more about how forest firefighters sometimes set blazes to stop wildfires and how you can prevent forest fires.

National Smokejumpers Association
www.smokejumpers.com
> Click on the Image Gallery link to see photos of smoke jumpers, their equipment, and their history.

Science News for Kids
www.sciencenewsforkids.org/articles/20060726/Note2.asp
> Learn how warmer weather may increase the number of forest fires.

Smokey Bear
www.smokeybear.com/kids/default.asp
> Play games, learn about forests, and find out how firefighters work.

INDEX

About the Author

William David Thomas lives in Rochester, New York, where he works with special-needs students. Bill has written software documentation, magazine articles, training programs, annual reports, books for children, a few poems, and lots of letters. He likes to go backpacking and canoeing, play his guitar, and obsess about baseball. Bill claims he was once King of Fiji but gave up the throne to pursue a career as a relief pitcher. It's not true.